CLICKBAIT

JAY SNODGRASS

2 0 1 5

ISBN 978-1508931065

For Kristine

The ossuary, diverged, silk line in polish, oak ready, bone coveted. Spring trees are immanent, having bent through a winter's meditation. The new buds cascade up, click the sky. Enter.

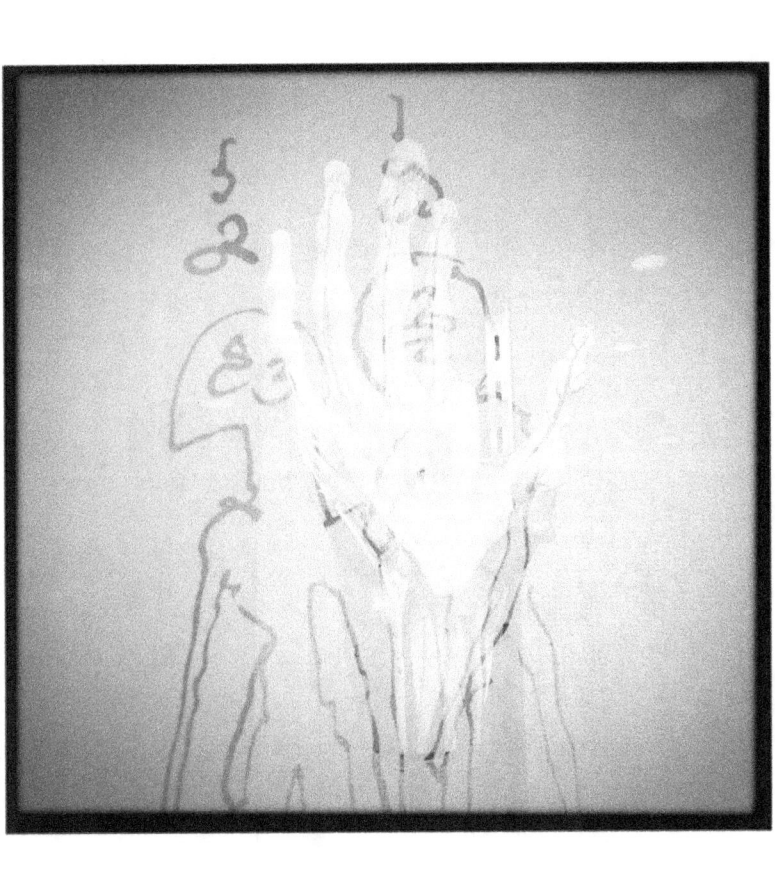

This strange arrangement, a grain, developing and ordinary.

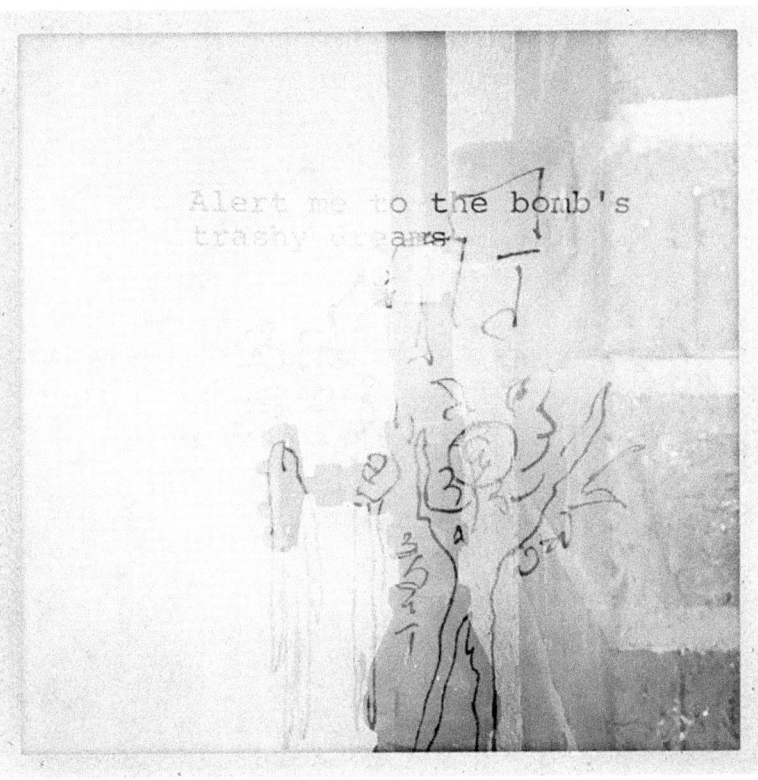

Lure, allure, the seizing of a cover, covert, time dimension, fractal knick knack, a doll's conviction, I have heart, a gift in this taste of sour medicine, order of plastic, borrowed mold, grieve.

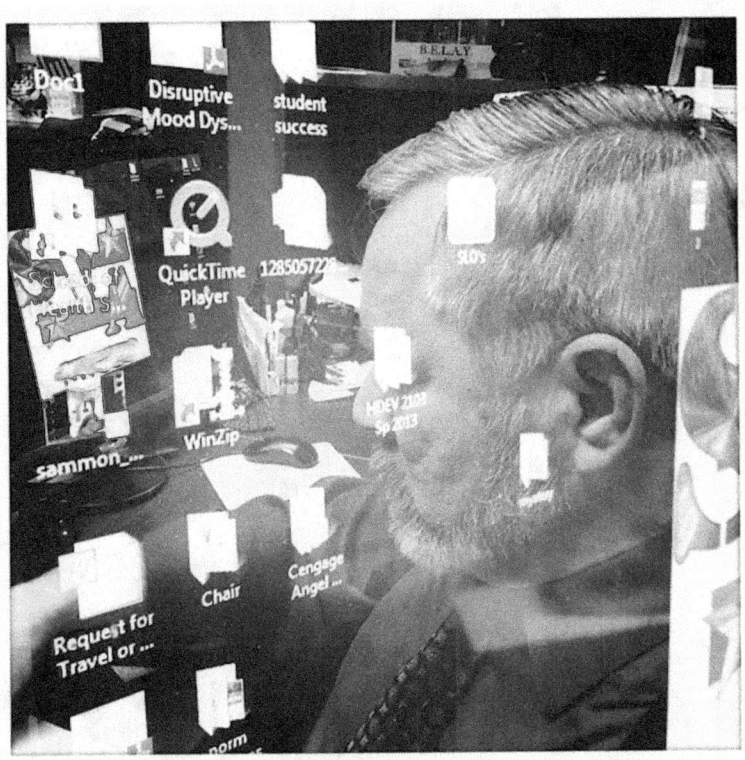

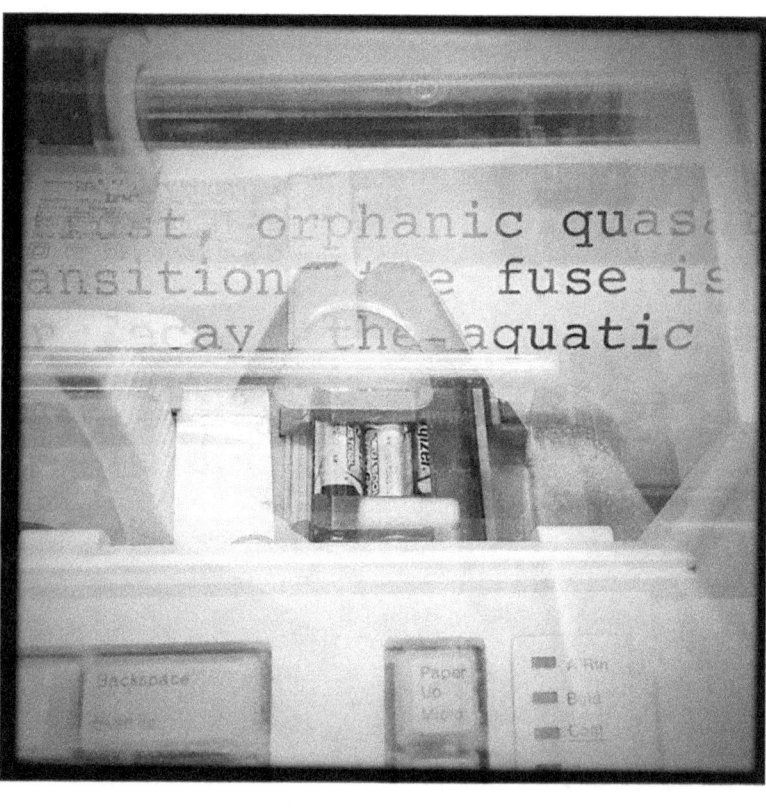

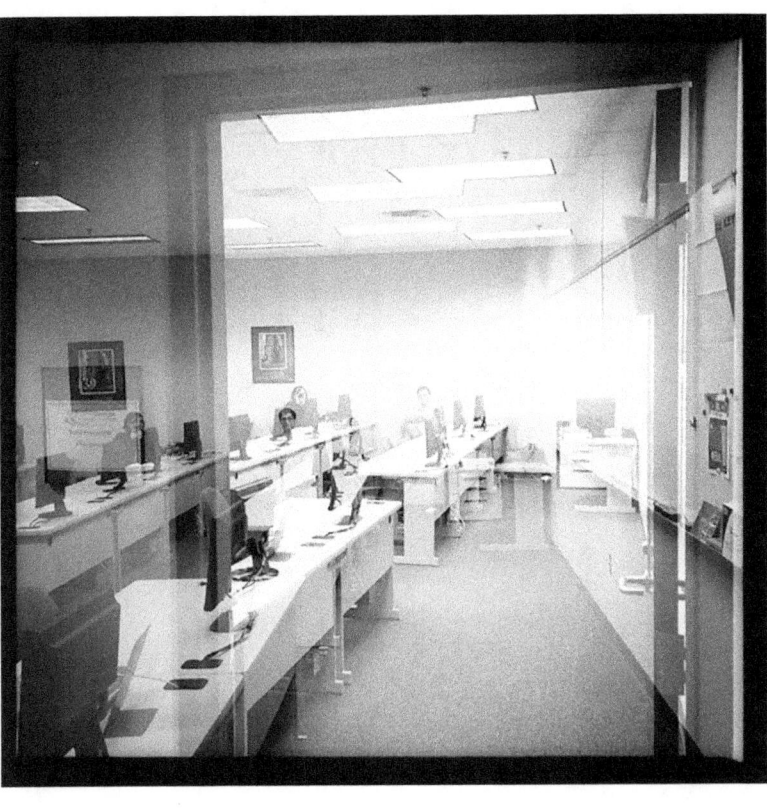

Soft color, sweet gasoline crops.
I sproputed a hand from the shallow dirt, collisions,
suppositions, round and joyful.

a horse.

Instead I am the horse

A soft cover, an eminent tipping, hassle and tassel of indicating. Click on this poison, soft and in question. And when there is an eye and arch to answer there will be supplements and preferences and take-aways and grace in a light blue.

Drift and brighten and claim a calamity. Change in to a great greyness, sky blind sheets and suits and laced in ivy.

The greeting is bound in strings and settled, in a red sound, a whole site to grind stores up from the sewn out timbers, careless, careless, careless.

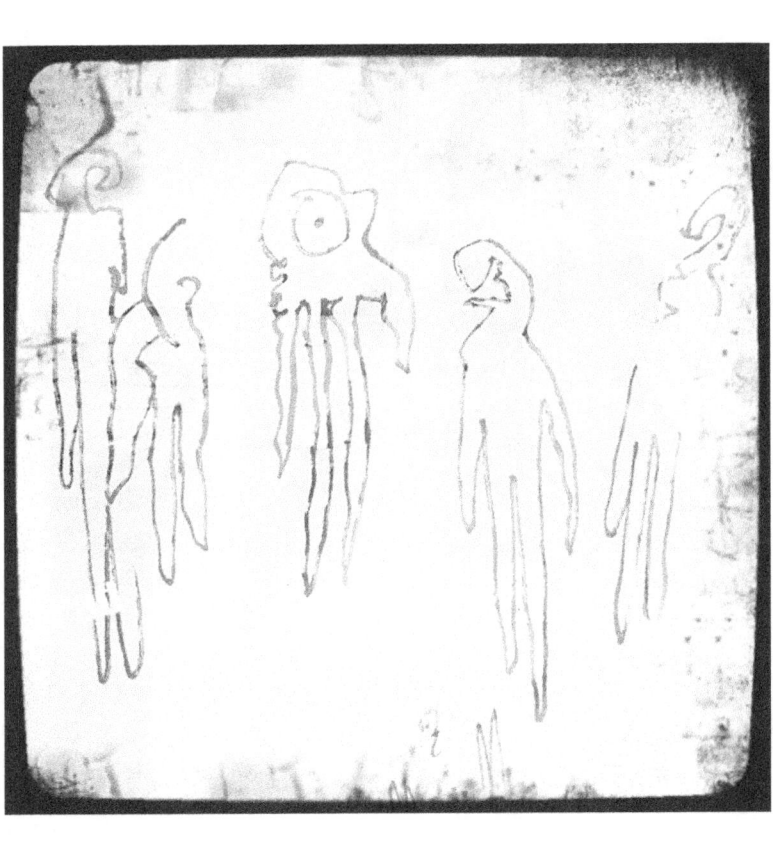

...ny, internal, ciphanic quasar
nd mistransition, the fuse is qui
over in decay, the aquatic mal

splendid, cracked a bit
d, v   for an instant
e   o e used, the frenzy
e   le dressed.

7 8

*

8

9

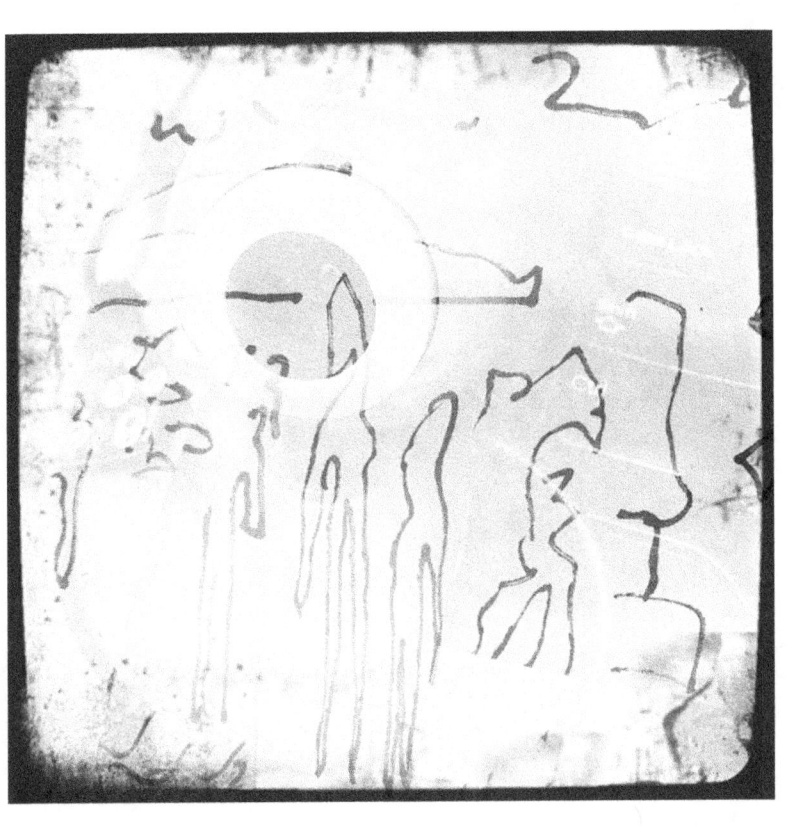

A salt and berry course upon the table, a row of plates bound in meats.

r

a   i   a

i   n   i

n   n

rain   rain

Words   like   upon

the canopy   of intrusion.

A disgrace of patience and a brown brick crumble, a cleared plane is bright with eyes, streaming from sap pores, tears on the hood, marbling sun ground to rounds.

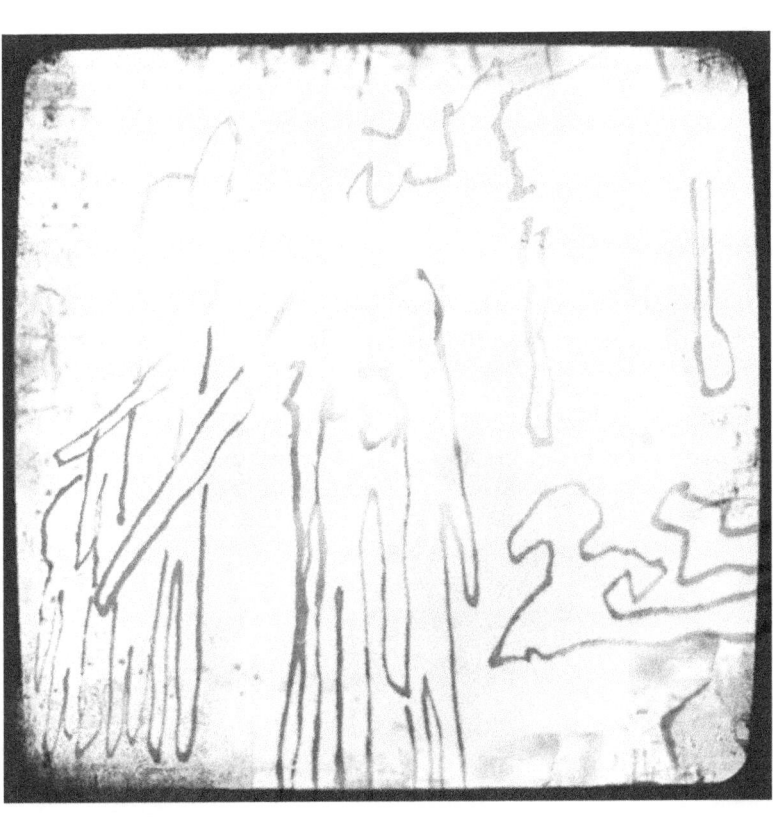

I had arisen, firm but fired from a coffee, a laugh, a chuff. This is not all there is, not even the picture. The walls have lips that gather dust which gathers mold wich grows in purpose like a smell. And a reason. The furniture also looms, late. A colonial wood, a laqured plastic hedge board. Distressed pants and a membrane, a website. Amazing.

Use of light and glitter, tongue custom, a soapy. A ribbon, tied, spooled, retired to a gift, a Holiday and heavy shaped niceness. Heavy.

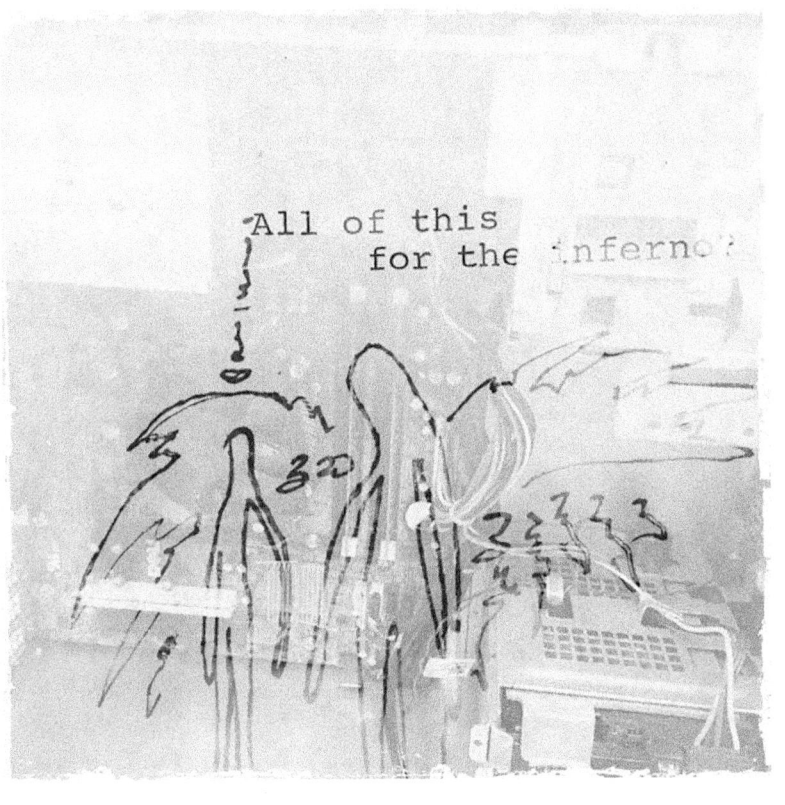

All of this
for the inferno?

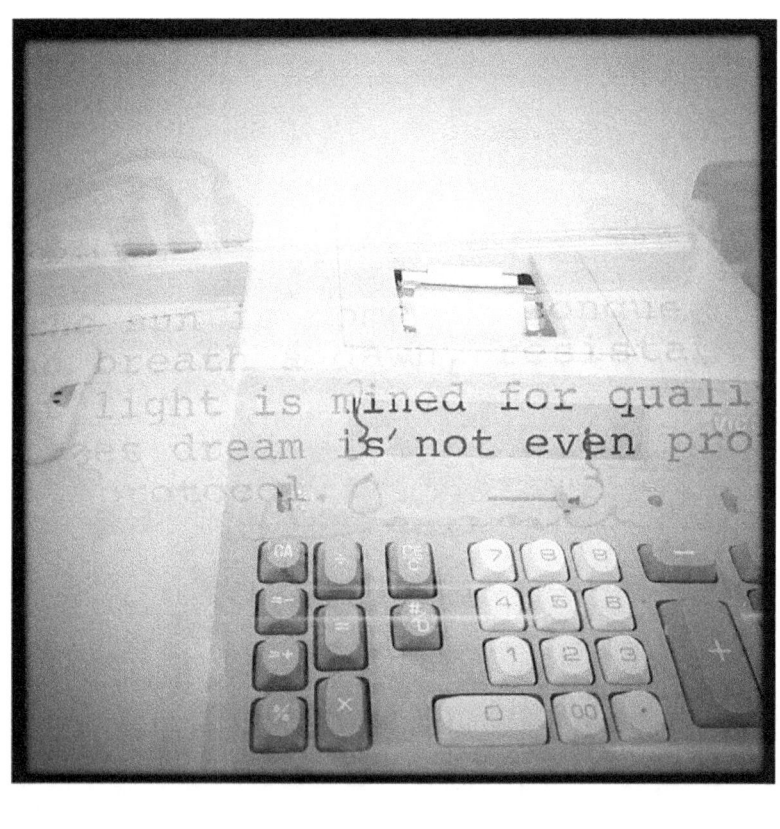

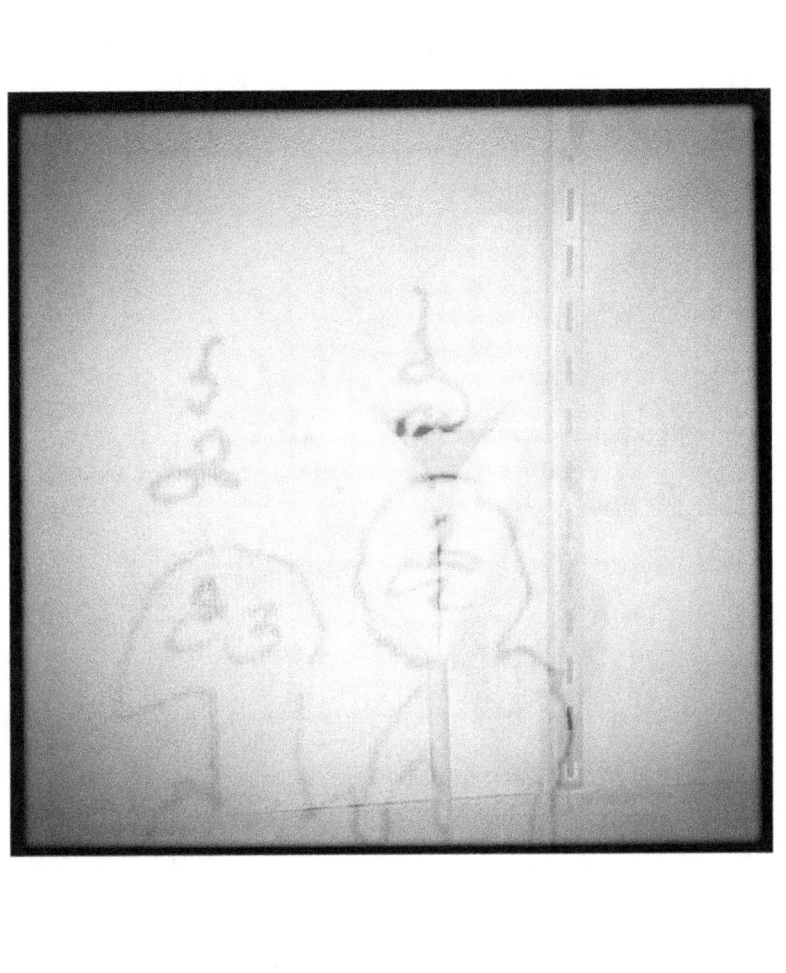

Passivity and melody and the length of a chair. And a fence in the yard and the mind with a flower arrangement in it become a garden and the change, there is serious.

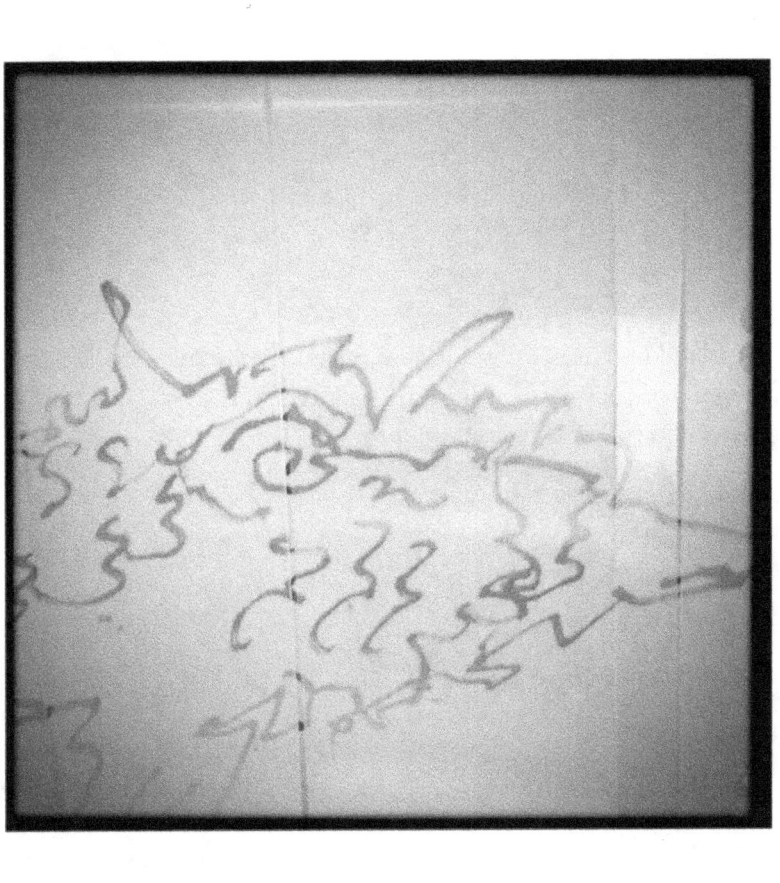

A rev and no release, surge and loud level, a small bag of cold food in the foot panel, a cold smell of egress, the escapists establishment, a cunning toss and return.

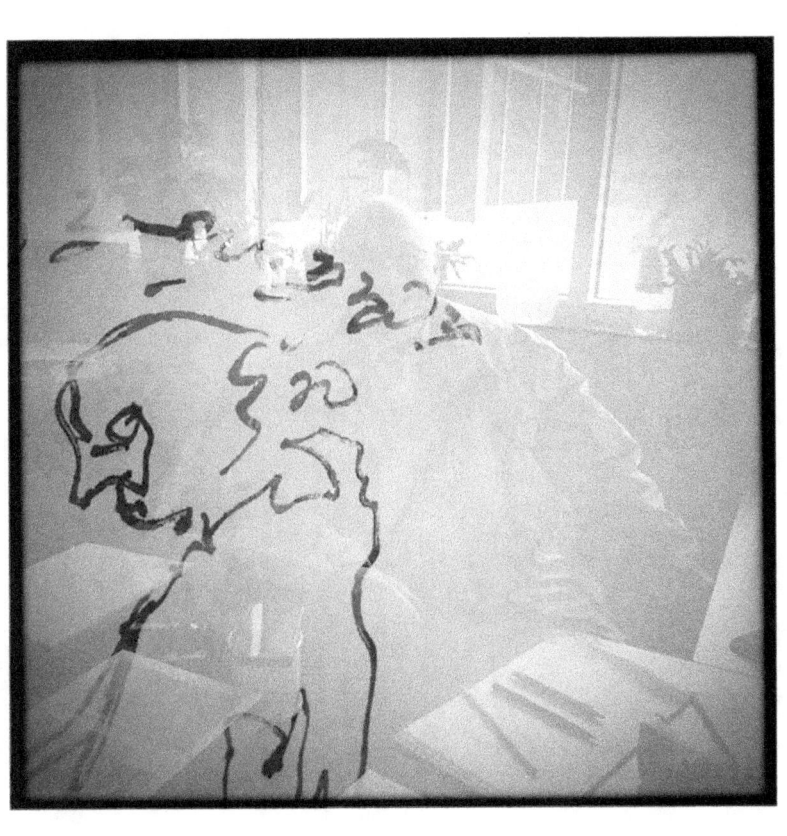

There is no line in all of this, the rope up a tree, and an adventure down a map's canyon lean, the way back is necessary, if this is the list of lines in the map.

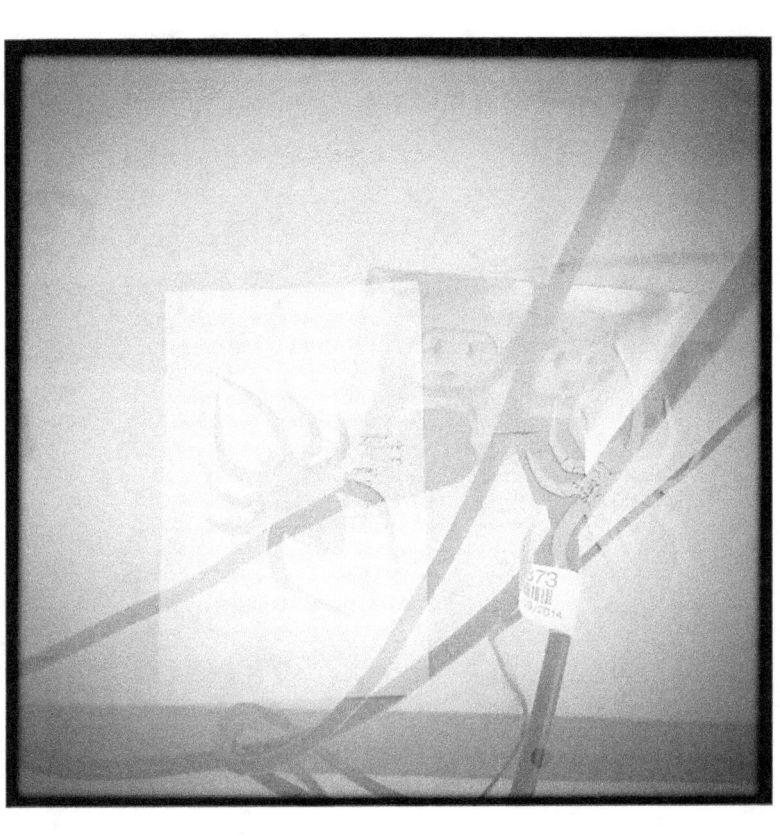

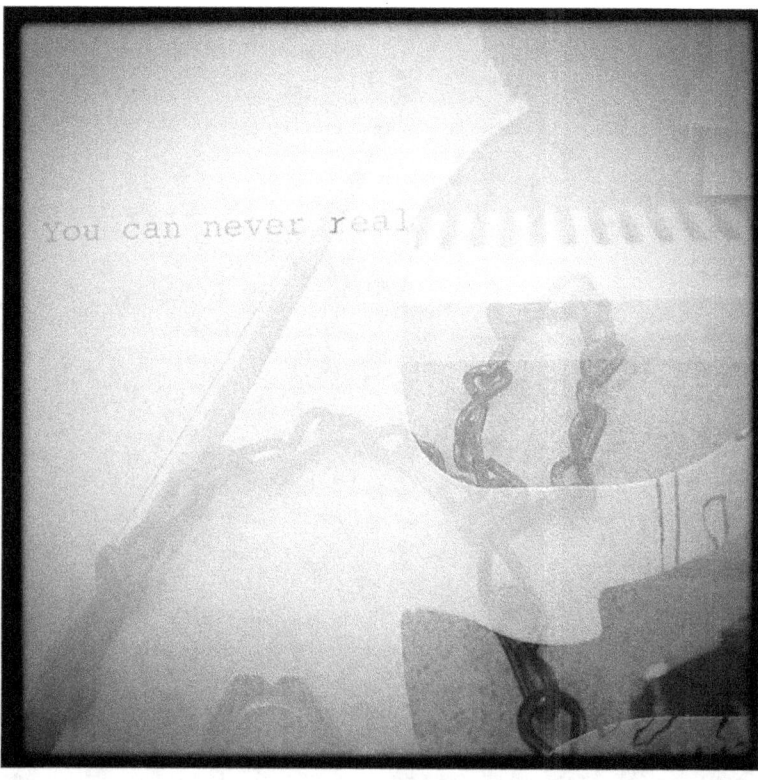

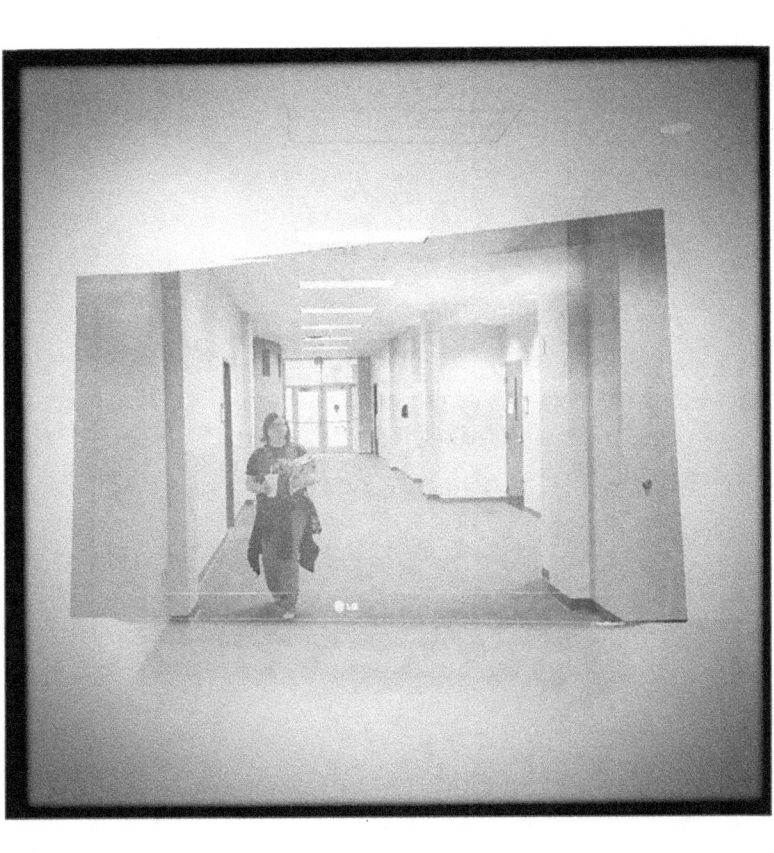

This is what you need to be needed to a flower fixed and to the car when it rolls out of silent gear by its own ghost. If you see this specter and are needed, it fixes you, a broken substance, planted result.

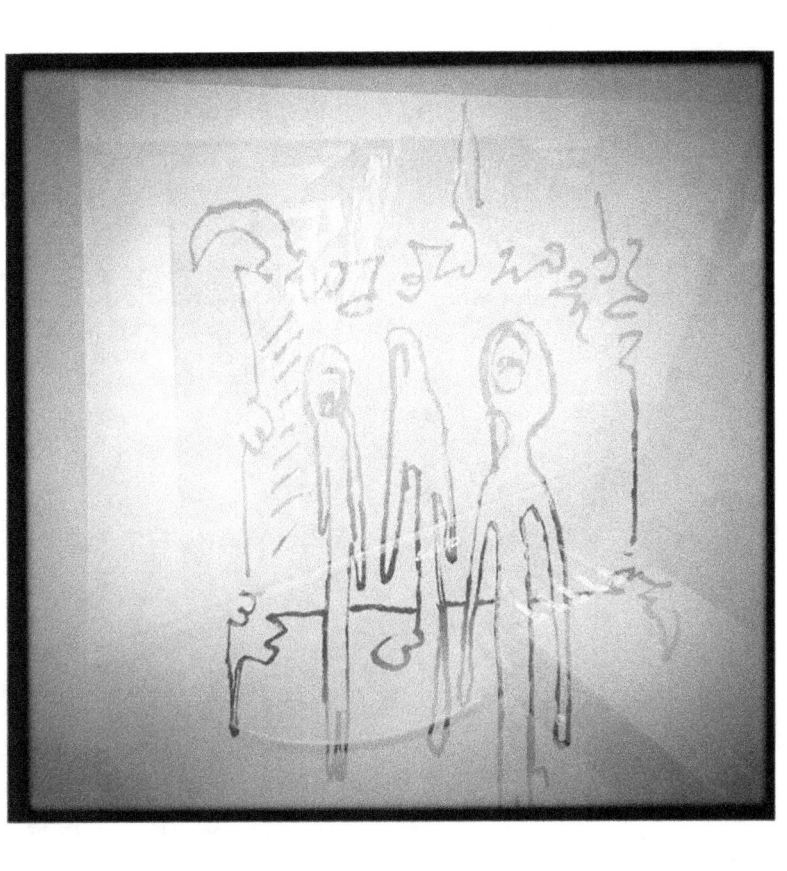

I had hopes before. The white gates of lilies, around the door, a yelp into frame, the knockout selfie, a grown corpse. This is the feeling, straight.

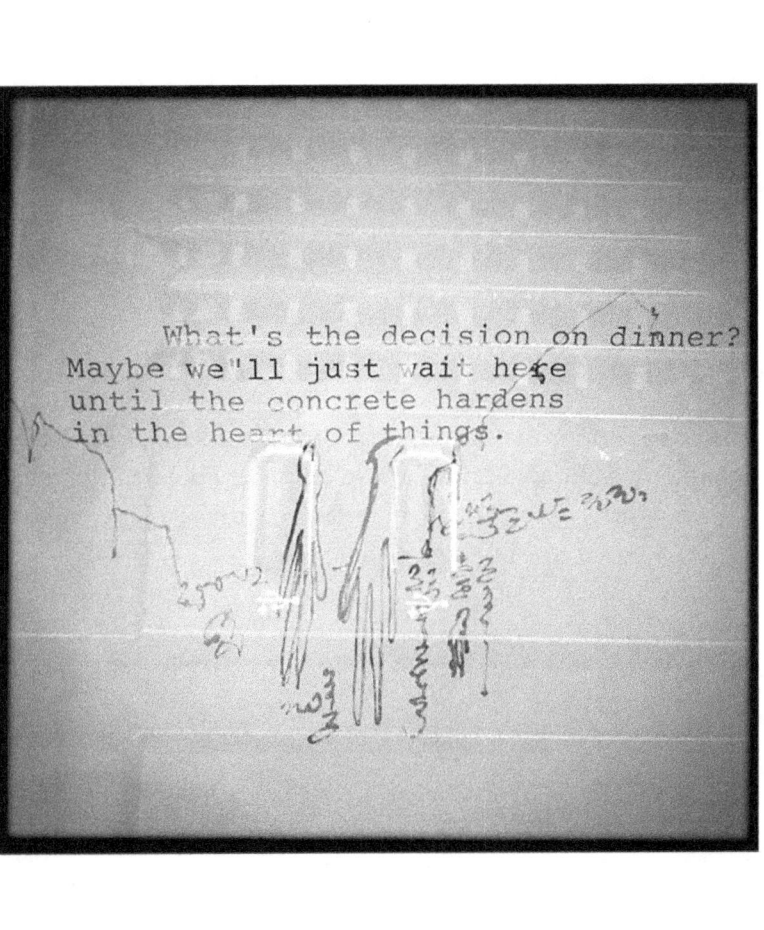

What's the decision on dinner?
Maybe we'll just wait here
until the concrete hardens
in the heart of things.

An end of light is the day, a line that edges the wild duck, the hallucinating cricket. I know how to say end stop. The beginning is a tenderness, un-breeze. The future sky is dark with growing. A blanket to cover, the privilege of not seeing.

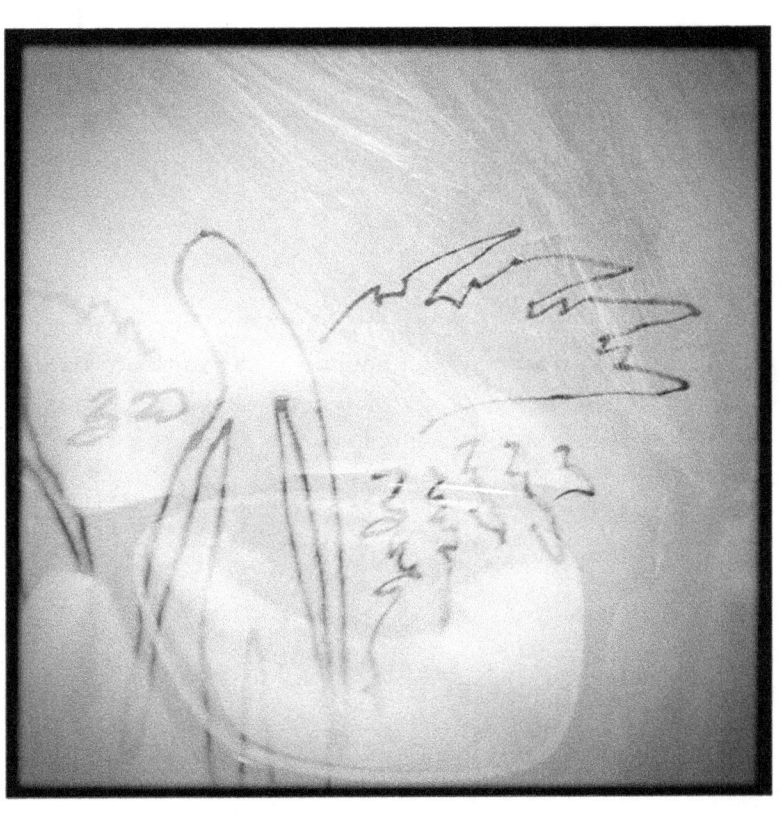

A cloud is as aware of itself as I am, diluted with city. As we are. The real, passing, to a tremble, tumultuous with castles, Wrapping these vents, these thistle grates with forgiven slipping. A fiction is a dawn too. A pulping of shadow. Each one is correct.

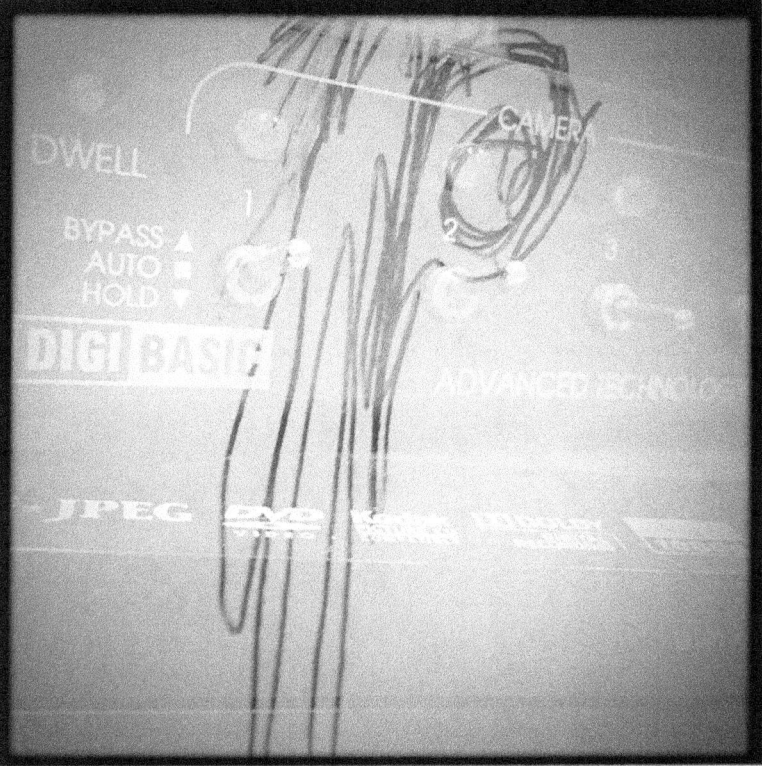

A beginning makes enough noise to break sure you want to close.

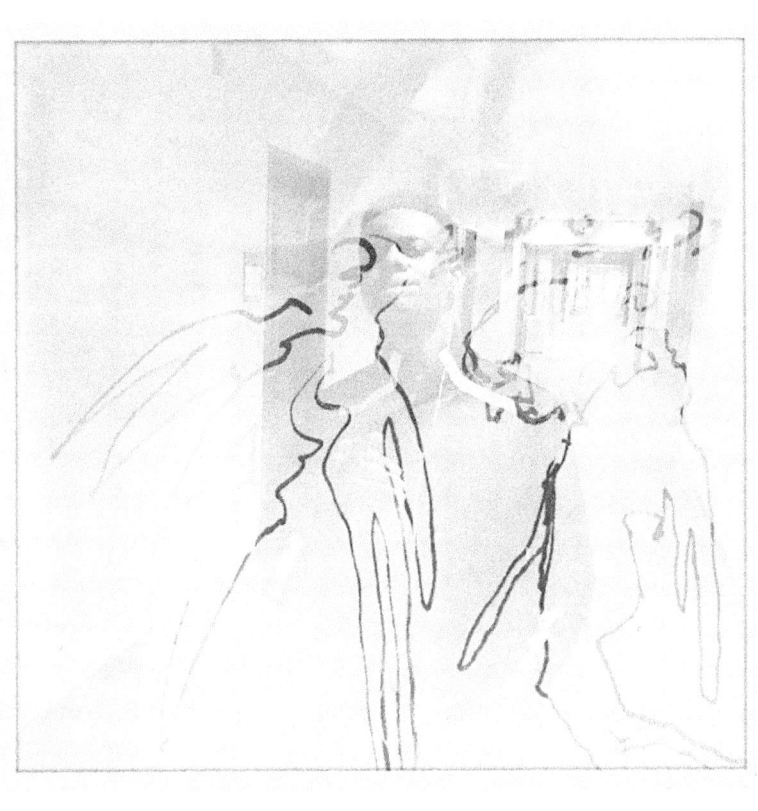